IMAGES
of England

AROUND
SPEKE

General view of comings and goings at Liverpool Airport, 1948. At that time the airport was only used by top businessmen and one or two other favoured passengers. The Dakota in the foreground tended to cater for the 'standard' traffic, whilst the bi-plane behind was generally used for charter flights and sight-seeing tours.

IMAGES
of England

AROUND
SPEKE

Compiled by
David Paul

TEMPUS

First published 1997, reprinted 1998, 2001
Copyright © David Paul, 1997

Tempus Publishing Limited
The Mill, Brimscombe Port,
Stroud, Gloucestershire, GL5 2QG

ISBN 0 7524 0798 8

Typesetting and origination by
Tempus Publishing Limited
Printed in Great Britain by
Midway Colour Print, Wiltshire

A three hundred year old cottage at Speke. (*Liverpool Daily Post* 14 June 1938) Speke Estate was purchased by Liverpool City Council from the trustees of the late Miss Adelaide Watt. The estate comprises 2,216 acres and cost about £200,000. That was in 1928, and it was decided not to create a suburban outgrowth from a neighbouring inhabited district, but a satellite town, with its own industrial area, recreation grounds, shopping centres, assembly hall and community centre, transport facilities and all the other amenities required for a self-contained unit with a population of about 25,000.

Contents

Acknowledgements

It has to be recorded that, without so many people who have given me so much assistance in several different ways, it would have been impossible to compile this collection of old photographs of Speke and its surrounding area. I am particularly indebted to my wife, Janet, my Mum, my sister, Jean, and to the many people associated with, or working in, the Central Library, Liverpool. I would especially like to thank Sylvia Bostock, Cllr Paul Bostock (Chair of the Libraries Committee, Liverpool City Council), David Stoker (Manager of the Liverpool Record Office) and all of the many, helpful, staff in the Local History section of the Central Library on the fourth floor.

Many other people gave me continued assistance, support and guidance, for which I am most grateful. In particular I would like to thank Mr and Mrs Puddifer who helped me to get started, Ian Mowat and Bill Frost who kept me going, and Mrs Lillian Redford who kindly loaned the last photographs for the collection. It would also be remiss of me not to make specific mention of Colin Kay, Joan McBride, Geraldine Dewberry, Beryl Jones, Ted Woodcock, Mrs Phyllis Alger and Mrs Adrienne Wright, all of whom helped in many different ways.

Finally, whilst I have made every endeavour to ensure that the notes are factually correct, any errors or inaccuracies are mine alone.

Introduction

When starting to delve into the history of the village community of Speke, and the Speke Estate which I knew as a child, many interesting facts came to my attention; for instance, the information that until the 1930s, the population of the village still numbered less than 400, but just a little more than twenty years later, the population numbered in excess of 25,000! This revolution is by far the most significant event in Speke's ancient history and changed for ever the complexion, composition and character of the town and the surrounding area. This collection of photographs, most of which have not been previously published, traces some of that developing history which the camera has managed to capture.

The name Speke is unique in England. Reference to the manor is included in Domesday as 'Spec'. The name has since been spelt in a variety of ways: 'Speek' appears in 1332, 'Speyke' in 1500, whilst in the sixteenth and seventeenth centuries the place was usually termed 'The Speke'. The name is believed to be derived from the Anglo-Saxon 'spic', denoting 'swine-pastures'. Similarly, the modern German *speck* (bacon) is from the same source and there is some evidence to support the claim that Speke was for many years a pig-breeding area.

In the thirteenth century the Manor of Speke was owned by the Molyneux family. Through marriage the estate passed to the Norris family. In 1490 Sir William Norris became lord of the manor and initiated the building of Speke Hall. Sometime later, the Beauclerk family owned the hall and estate until it was sold to Richard Watt in 1795 for a purchase price of £75,500. The estate was passed on to succeeding generations of the Watt family until the last incumbent, Miss Watt, succeeded to the property and estate in 1865 when her father, Richard Watt, was tragically killed in an accident. At that time, the young Adelaide was only eight years old. Until she was twenty-one, the estate was administered by her trustees. Miss Watt died on 21 August 1921, the Hall and estate being left in trust. In 1928 the trustees of her estate sold much of the land to Liverpool Corporation - 'a wonderful riverside estate in the heart of green fields sloping to the banks of the River Mersey' for the 'absurd' price of £200,000! The city architect was commissioned to draw up plans for a self-contained satellite town, which was to be designed to house a population of approaching 25,000 - very different from the size of the village population.

The original concept was to build a satellite town with an 'Air Port' adjacent to it. Work went ahead and on 1 July 1933, 'one of the finest aeroplane landing-grounds in England' was opened as an 'Air Port' by the Marquis of Londonderry, Secretary of State for Air. The airport, as described by Mr W.C. Rule, deputy surveyor for the city council at the time, 'is a square area, with sides some three-quarters of a mile long'. Meanwhile the city planners and architects had designed the new satellite town and focussed very much on the advantages offered by the water front location. This aspect had not been forgotten by the airport authorities and they had plans to build a base for sea planes when demand for air services developed. Already a new concept in flying had been pioneered at Speke Airport, as it was becoming colloquially known: the air taxi service. 'The corporation have made arrangements whereby air-taxis are available at a few minutes' notice for journeys of any length. A four-seater enclosed machine can be hired for 1s (5p) a mile for the double journey, or 3d (1½p) per mile per passenger, and a single-seater for 9d (4p) per mile.' In fact, the early days of the airport, or 'Air Port' or 'Aerodrome', were very exciting times.

Some little time before work was due to commence on the new town, the Air Ministry announced that it was to commission and build a 'shadow' aircraft production facility. Originally, twenty-three possible sites had been considered for the factory. A final choice was made and plans went ahead to build it at Maidenhead. However, because of high rates of unemployment in Liverpool, coupled with an opportunity for general economic rejuvenation, the city council decided to make a last ditch attempt to have the factory constructed in the city. Following some further developments at the Air Ministry and intense collaboration between Rootes Securities Ltd, who would produce the aircraft on behalf of the Air Ministry, the Speke Estate (Special) Sub-Committee, corporation staff and local farmers, a radical reappraisal of the site was precipitated and, eventually, the Air Ministry opted for Speke.

On 15 February 1937 the Lord Mayor of Liverpool, Alderman W. Denton and Sir Thomas White, Chairman of the Speke Estate (Special) Sub-Committee, performed the ceremonial opening of the site for the proposed shadow aircraft factory. It was estimated that the factory would cost £500,000 to build, and would be the largest factory in Europe at that time, which, when operating at full productive capacity, would employ in excess of 5,000 workers. The lord mayor, in his address said of the proposed factory: 'It is so full of possibilities...the beginning of the industrial prosperity for which Liverpool has been waiting so long.' A civic blessing for the occasion had been written by the Dean of Liverpool which included the sentence, 'This day is to Liverpool a day of new beginnings, wherein our city shall be refreshed by new resources for honest labour, whereby the four winds of Heaven may be furnished with wings of wisdom to bind the Furies and with the wings of sincerity to give assurance of peace.'

Back to the drawing board! Plans for Speke as originally conceived and passed by the city council now had to be redrawn. All of the proposed amenities with which the new town would be blessed were retained; in fact, the new plans, with their shift in focus, now incorporated a wide boulevard leading through the Dam Wood to the river's edge, where a promenade would be built together with a salt water, open-air swimming pool. Other amenities planned included a technical college, numerous schools, shopping centres, churches, a community centre, cinemas, recreation grounds and a public golf course. A spokesman for the housing department of the Liverpool Corporation said, 'The estate has been planned so as to accommodate all classes of the community, thus avoiding the segregation of one class, a condition which is now widely recognised as a deterrent to social progress. The proposals therefore are for a self-contained community unit rather than for a dormitory estate for occupation only by the lower paid workers.'

The history and development of the area - from being the tiny village of Speke, through to the village being transformed into a satellite town, have been traced through the pages of this book. Although history, as it has been traditionally taught, tends to be about castles, queens, kings, governments, politics and battles, it is also about the lives of ordinary people - their homes, their places of work, their pleasures and pastimes, and also, importantly, their families and friends. This book is about the people of Speke and the area nearby. Many of the photographs have been taken from the vast collection in the Liverpool Record Office, Liverpool Central Library. Others have been given by individuals, most of whom are still living in Speke.

David Paul
May 1997

8

One
The Village of Speke

Speke Station in its heyday! The station was opened on 1 July 1852 and was very busy for many years but later, due to lack of passenger demand, the station was closed on 22 September 1930. The Parsonage on Woodend Lane, (later renamed Woodend Avenue) can be seen behind the station.

View from the platform level showing the bridge carrying Woodend Lane (later renamed Woodend Avenue) from Hunts Cross to Speke. The station had been closed for six years when this photograph was taken on 8 June 1936.

Many of the original cottages from the village of Speke were still standing as late as 1954 when this photograph was taken. Building work on the new estate of Speke continued for many years to come.

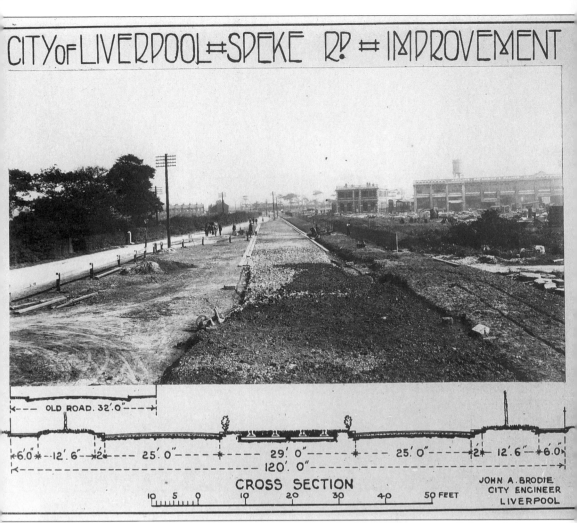

CITY OF LIVERPOOL ⇌ SPEKE R? ⇌ IMPROVEMENT

OLD ROAD. 32'. 0"

6.0" — 12'. 6" — 2" — 25'. 0" — 29'. 0" — 25'. 0" — 2" — 12'. 6" — 6.0"

120'. 0"

CROSS SECTION

10 5 0 10 20 30 40 50 FEET

JOHN A. BRODIE
CITY ENGINEER
LIVERPOOL

Speke Road, 14 September 1921. This road, seen here under construction, will lead to the satellite town of Speke. It was anticipated that when the town was built it would house some 25,000 people. On the right in the background can be seen the match works, Bryant & May.

Speke Road Bridge under construction, October 1921. The view looks towards the village of Garston, which at that time, was right on the outskirts of the city of Liverpool. The road running to the right is Horrocks Avenue.

Speke Road a few years later, 8 May 1928. Looking from the outskirts of Garston the road to the new satellite town at Speke has now been completed. The main building programme was scheduled to commence shortly after.

Dodds Lane was the road which linked Speke with Garston - and civilisation! Because the road skirted the airport runway, special lights had to be installed so as not to distract any pilots during landing.

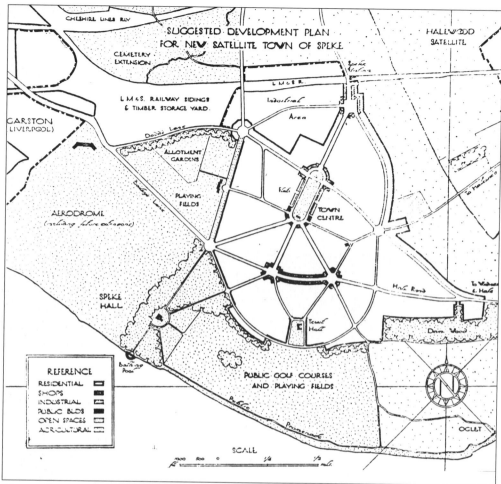

The satellite town of Speke as originally envisaged by the city's planners and architects in 1937. It was proposed that the town would be located much nearer to the River Mersey with a public golf course edging the banks of the river and an open air swimming pool, but, due to a central government initiative to build an industrial complex near the town, the plans were significantly modified. Needless to say, when the town was built just after the end of the Second World War, many of the planned leisure and social facilities were not built.

All Saints Church from Hale Road, 10 December 1934. At this time, before the building of the town had been started, the population of the village of Speke was just under 400 souls!

The River Mersey at Dungeon - its widest point. Until the turn of the century it was possible to navigate large ships up the river as far as Hale. Many took their last trip up the Mersey to the breaker's yard at Dungeon.

The church hall at All Saints Church, Speke. The story is still told in Speke that Leonard Rossiter started his acting career here. Apparently, on practice and rehearsal nights he used to wait outside for his girlfriend who was a member of the Speke Amateur Dramatic Group. On becoming tired of waiting one evening he went in to see exactly what was happening, and, as they say, the rest is history!

Plans for the satellite town of Speke had to be considerably modified because of the building of a large factory, Rootes (later Dunlop's). However, a number of houses had already been built. In 1938 some houses along Hale Road had even been built with garages! This was certainly a break with tradition for corporation-built houses - even though there were very few privately owned cars in Speke at that time. The familiar spire of All Saints Church can be seen to the left in the background.

Walking to church along Speke Town Lane on a cold winter's day. One of the cottages was later used as a temporary clinic so that mothers from Speke could collect their dried baby milk rather than having to traipse all the way to the clinic in Garston.

Hale Cliffs at the bottom of Dungeon Lane in 1949. Sometime before this, the Mersey was a well known shrimping bed. Women carried baskets of shrimps across the fields to Garston market.

On 23 February 1937 there was a farm sale at Hale Road Farm, Speke - the farm belonging to Mr Alfred Sumner, seen in the inset. The main auction scene took place in one of the farm sheds. All of the sheds and implements from the farm were sold at the auction so that everything could be cleared for the building of the new aircraft factory.

The very next day, 24 February 1937, work started on clearing the ground to start building the new aircraft factory.

Speke Town Lane, Speke. Amid the thousands of modern houses built at Speke stands this little white washed, half timbered, four roomed cottage, a lonely link with the brave days of old. The cottage dates back to 1631. Its present occupants are Mr John Ireland and his niece, Mrs Frances J. Raper, who have lived there most of their lives. Mr Ireland, in keeping with the age of his home, proclaims himself to be one of the oldest men of Speke, if not the oldest. He is 87. Mrs Raper is 75. (*Evening Express*, 3 November 1944)

The old Parsonage in Woodend Lane. From here, on the outskirts of Speke, the vicar could travel directly to the church which was in the centre of the village. Later, when the new road was built and renamed Woodend Avenue, the Parsonage became known as the Bank House. It was owned by the National Provincial Bank and used as a branch office.

Dungeon Wood as it was in 1950 - a rich play area for the children of the village and the newly developing estate of Speke. A runway for the airport was built through this wood sometime later.

Home Farm Cottages, Speke, October 1964.

An old photograph of some of the cottages along Speke Town Lane. Most of the cottages relied upon the traditional thatched roofs, but, as can be seen, some began using slate instead.

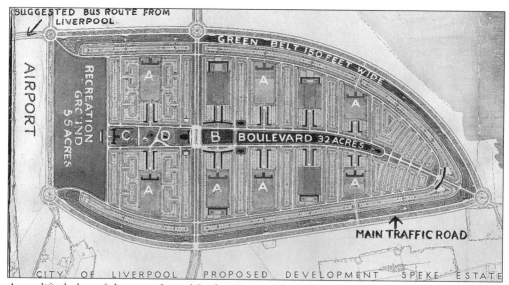

A modified plan of the township of Speke. Even at this stage, in late 1936, although the plans were being continuously modified, the concept of the satellite town was still intact. This plan incorporated a large recreation ground and several other green areas.

On 9 September 1937, Liverpool's Director of Housing, Mr L.H. Keay, had his amended and enlarged layout for the proposed £2,000,000 satellite town approved by the Liverpool Housing Committee. Amongst other amenities, the proposed town boasted a technical college, numerous schools, shopping centres, churches, a community centre, cinemas, recreation grounds, a public golf course and an open-air swimming pool.

A family photograph of the Sumners taken in their back garden in Speke Town Lane at the turn of the century; Mr and Mrs Sumner owned the post office. They had five children, which was not unusual in those days.

Old Hutte Lane in 1948. When the estate of Speke was built, this lane became Eastern Avenue, one of Speke's main roads.

Another photograph taken in the Sumner's back garden, just before the family walked down to All Saints Church for the wedding of their daughter. She was to marry a man from Hale, just a few miles away.

The bride and groom together with the best man, groomsman and bridesmaids. The wedding was held at All Saints Church in 1920.

The bride and groom after the wedding.

Another Sumner family wedding.

Standing proudly outside their home in Speke Town Lane are Mrs Sumner and two of her five children. The family owned the original post office in Speke and were also 'carters'. This photograph was taken in the early 1920s, as can be seen from the style of the lady's hat!

A 1952 aerial view of Speke looking eastwards. The road running across the centre of picture and over the main Liverpool-London railway line is Speke Hall Road. At the right end of this road is the new roundabout. Leading from this and moving towards the top of the picture, Speke Boulevard is being constructed. The factory of Brown, Bibby & Gregory can be seen to the left of the boulevard. The marshalling yard in the foreground was taken over in 1948 by British Railways when the railways were nationalised. The road running upwards from the bottom left is Goodlass Road.

In March 1938, the township of Speke was just a few roads with houses, as can be seen from this aerial view. On the extreme right is the bend in the dual carriageway on Speke Hall Avenue. Just to the left of that can be seen All Saints Church, with Hale Road going away towards the top of the picture. The road under construction to the mid-left of the view is Speke Boulevard. Neither Western Avenue nor any of the houses on that side of Speke have yet been built.

Two
Building Commences

During the early years of building, the horse and cart were very much in evidence. There wasn't very much industrial plant to speak of in 1938! The Morris van, seen just behind the horse, was owned by Smith's of Garston. Smith's was the best toy shop there, and quite a few children from Speke were aware of its wonders!

The days are numbered for the old cottages in Speke Town Lane. Work has now started on laying the foundations for the new Speke Housing Estate. Workmen are seen here on 7 April 1938, laboriously laying the foundations for the new walkway, as the new houses will be built just behind.

Architects check plans and foundations are dug as work begins on the new boulevard road at Speke. The new roadway, which will eventually be the widest thoroughfare in the country, begins at the large roundabout near Speke Hall and will join up with the new Liverpool-Widnes road at the county boundary.

Church Road, Speke. On the left are newly erected houses and on the right are the old houses due to be demolished under the new housing schemes. (*Liverpool Daily Post*, 16 August 1938)

Even in 1952, when this photograph was taken, the Speke Estate, as it was now known, was still very much in its infancy. The old smithy on the right has now been converted to a public library and some of the cottages in Speke Town Lane are still standing.

Infrastructure work for the satellite town started shortly after the original plans were passed. Workmen are seen here in July 1936 laying foundations for the town's main sewerage system.

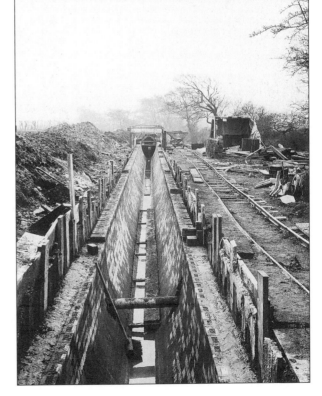

As the satellite town was designed for a population of some 25,000, extensive infrastructure building was needed before any work could begin on the houses and other social amenities. This work was interrupted by the Second World War and was not completed until long after 1945.

Work on the Oglet outfall continuing in February 1949. Speke Estate was still in its infancy.

Workmen contemplating the job ahead. The foundation work on the Speke outfall took many years to complete.

Building commences on some of the first houses to be built on the Speke Estate. Many of the early houses were built in blocks of four or five dwellings, sometimes even more!

Pictured in the *Liverpool Post* on 1 November 1937, 'the first block of the 300 houses now being constructed by the Liverpool Corporation on the Speke Estate. Rapid changes are taking place in the countryside in this area.'

The new township of Speke begins to take shape. Taken in November 1937, this scene shows the building of some of the first houses in the town. (*Liverpool Daily Post*, 20 April 1938)

In August 1949 major work was still scheduled for the Oglet outfall.

Extensive changes had to be made all along the road when the dual carriageway was built at Woodend Avenue. The road had previously been a single carriageway when it was Woodend Lane and lead to All Saints Church. The girder and gantry are seen being placed in position - a very delicate task.

Three
Speke Estate

By 1953 Speke was becoming more established. A new bus terminus had been opened at the bottom of Eastern Avenue. The No.82E went right along Western Avenue before turning left and making its precarious way down the pot-holed Hale Road; it took another left turn into Eastern Avenue and then went right along to the terminus at the end of the road. The bus shown here is passing the 'Little Woods' as they were known colloquially, on its way back to the city centre.

As can be seen from this shot of Hale Road, there was no pavement to speak of and it was difficult for buses to pass each other with ease. As the bus route was becoming increasingly important to the well being and development of Speke, the argument to improve the road was very convincing.

In 1955 serious consideration was being given to widening Hale Road. The city engineer and surveyor's department assessed the traffic flow and came to the conclusion that the road did in fact need to be broadened.

One of the 'prefab' sites in Speke. These houses are located in Clough Road. The Lockheed factory can be seen in the background to the right. There were other 'prefab' roads at Rycot Road and also in the Dymchurch area of the estate.

Model of the proposed new Anglican church of St Aidan, which was to form the centrepiece of the development plans for Speke, 9 June 1953.

As Speke developed and became more established, further infrastructure building became necessary. This is the Liverpool Corporation Passenger Transport Garage built in 1955.

Once the houses were built and the estate became more established, the post-war baby boom hit Speke. Seen here, children cross Western Avenue at Stapleton Avenue on their way home from Stocktonwood Road School.

Trees began to grow in Western Avenue as the area became more established. The road surface is still the same as it was immediately after the war, when tarmac was at a premium. The house immediately behind the telephone box, to the right of the photograph, is No. 72 Western Avenue, where Sir Paul McCartney spent much of his early childhood and youth.

View looking up Western Avenue from the 'Pegasus end'. In the distance, right at the very top of Western Avenue, can be seen the factory belonging to Evans Medical Supplies Ltd.

Stapleton Avenue. Many types of houses were built in Speke in order to fulfil the varying requirements of different families. Some houses, as can be seen here, were specially designed for larger families.

The junction of Western Avenue and Tarbock Road. Speke really did have a wide variety of different types of dwellings.

The road from Garston to Speke, which was started in 1921, was Speke Road Gardens. The tenements, which were built many years after the road was constructed, can be seen on the far side of the road. Just out of the picture, on the left of the road is the match works owned by Bryant & May, another major employer in the area for many years. The match works, the last in England, ceased production on 23 December 1994.

The top end of Western Avenue. The houses on the left are at the start of Bray Road. Some of the 'prefabs' in Rycot Road can be seen behind the lamp post on the right of the scene.

A block of three-storey terraced houses in Speke. Originally, when 'social engineering' was scheduled to play a significant role in the development and establishment of the satellite town, these houses were designed for managers in industry who perhaps needed extra space for entertaining or continuing to work at home.

The Crescent was the first purpose-built block of shops in Speke. Mobile shops were still very much the way of shopping, even as late as the mid-fifties.

The other side of Waterworths in the Crescent. For many children in Speke, one of the regular jobs at the weekend was to help with the Saturday shopping - a mixed blessing for parents!

The Upper School, Speke County Comprehensive School, Central Avenue, 27 January 1975. 'Flares' were very much in fashion.

The far side of Speke County Comprehensive School, Central Avenue, 27 January 1975.

Aerial view of Speke showing in the foreground: Alderwood County Primary School, in the centre, All Hallows Roman Catholic Secondary Modern School and, in the background, the newly-built Ford factory.

Aerial view of Speke looking north west. By 1952 there were significant changes in the landscape of the town. The road running from the centre left border to the roundabout is Western Avenue, and the road from the roundabout up to the top right corner is Woodend Avenue.

Speke Central Library opened in October 1956. Many of the house building projects had been completed and the builder's attention was now turning to the construction of shops, churches and other social amenities such as the Central Library which, as its name implies, was right at the very centre of the estate.

Inside, the library was well stocked and was certainly not short of borrowers!

Speke Estate was an important development in that it was planned as early as 1936 as a complex township to be developed in its entirety by the Council. Building began in 1937 and was completed by about 1953. It combined houses, flats, an industrial estate and ancillary buildings, and was intended for a balance of population of all ages.

The official opening ceremony of the Speke Recreation Ground.

The Lord Mayor of Liverpool opened the Speke Recreation Ground in 1958, and then went on to demonstrate his prowess with the bat. Seen in the background are some of the 'prefabs' which had been erected in the Dymchurch area of the estate.

Every house built in Speke had both a front and back garden. This was something new for many of the families who were moving to the town from the inner city. The City Council organised competitions to find the *Best Kept Garden*. As can be seen here, there was immense pride in looking after the garden and a degree of friendly rivalry between neighbours.

There were many different categories in the Best Kept Garden competition. In 1958 this row of houses, Nos 149-55 Hale Road, won the collective prize for the best kept group of gardens.

Four
Speke Hall

Speke Hall in snow.

Children from Speke playing in the grounds of Speke Hall. Many children walked out to the Hall for an afternoon of fun and games.

Roy Kinnear in a film scene being shot at Speke Hall. Actors from films and television plays are often to be found on location here.

Speke Hall.

The Lord Mayor of Liverpool, accompanied by the Lady Mayoress and other councillors, made an official visit to Speke Hall on 6 November 1943. At that time Speke Hall and the Speke Hall Estate were owned by the City Council.

Speke Hall, May 20th 1878.

In Celebration of the Coming of Age of Miss Watt.

MENU

SOUP
MOCK TURTLE.

FISH
SALMON.

ENTREES
VEAL CUTLETS.   COMPOTE OF PIGEONS.

REMOVES
BOILED CHICKENS AND TONGUE.   BRAISED BEEF.

ROASTS
LAMB   DUCKLINGS.

ENTREMETS
PLUM PUDDINGS.   JELLIES.
CREAMS   FRENCH PASTRY.

ICES
ICE PUDDING.

DESSERT

When Miss Adelaide Watt, owner of Speke Hall, 'achieved her majority', there were celebrations throughout the estate. Special dinners were held. This is the menu from one of those grand occasions.

The Passing of Adelaide Watt.

1921

On Sunday, August 21st, at 3-45 p.m. Adelaide Watt, of Speke Hall, Lancashire, and Spott House, Haddingtonshire, passed peacefully away into the unseen world at the age of 64. For several years she had been in failing health, but the end came with almost tragic suddenness. On Saturday morning she appeared much as usual, but about noon she complained of feeling unwell. The doctor was soon in attendance, but she became rapidly worse, and on Sunday morning the Specialist who had been summoned, held out no hope. Major Hudson telephoned for the Canon, who arrived at the Hall at 3 p.m. and held a Commendatory Service. A few minutes later —3-45 p.m.—the passing of the Lady of Speke Manor took-place. Miss Watt succeeded to the Speke Estate on the death of her father, the late Richard Watt. She was a minor at the time and was brought up by her uncle, Mr. Sprott, of Spott House, Dunbar, which, on his death, she inherited. Miss Watt lived a secluded life, mingling little in Society, engrossed in the management of her large estates, in which she took the most profound interest. No one could possibly have worked harder or more conscientiously, most of the hours of every day being spent in dealing with her voluminous correspondence. When the livings of Garston and Speke fell vacant she took an infinitude of trouble in nominating the men whom she considered the right men to fill the vacancies. And nothing gave her more pleasure when the Bishop, approving her choice, conferred the honour of a Canonry in the Liverpool Cathedral on the Vicar of Garston. Her benefactions to the Parish of Garston have been many and varied, and Garston has lost a generous patron, and the Vicar a gracious and considerate friend. She will be much missed. For almost half a century the Lady of Speke Manor has gone in and out amongst her people, doing countless acts of sympathy and kindness to many whom we know not of. Who that ever knew her can ever forget her charming personality. her delicious speaking voice, her keen intellect, her cultured, even ascetic countenance, her spare form, bowed and burdened with the weight of the immense responsibility of the administration of her large estates. On St. Bartholomew's Day a Memorial Eucharist was held at Speke Church, followed by cremation at Anfield, and on Thursday (August 25th) an impressive service took place, when the "ashes" of Adelaide Watt were laid to rest in the sanctuary ; the officiating clergy being the Rev. L. R. Paterson, Vicar of Speke, the Rev. Canon Rowe, Vicar of Garston, and the Rev. J. D. Bruce, Vicar of Dunbar,— the Dean of York (Venerable Foxley Norris)—being among the congregation. On Sunday (Aug. 28th) Memorial Services were held in the Parish Church, the Canon preaching morning and evening. The flag was half-mast, and muffled peals were rung. At the conclusion of each service, the "Dead March" was played.

When Miss Watt died in 1921, an extremely sober and respectful article was written in the parish magazine of St Michael's, Garston. Although Miss Watt had built All Saints Church in the village of Speke, not too far away from Speke Hall, she still attended, on a regular basis, the church in the neighbouring parish - perhaps preferring a more established church community.

Speke Hall.

Five
Liverpool (Speke) Airport

Surface laying begins on the new West High Speed taxiway, Liverpool Airport, 31 January 1966. This was to be one of the longest runways in Europe. The Thames Trader Tipper, seen on the runway, was one of the most popular lorries of the day and much in evidence during the period of construction.

In February 1937 building work started on the new control tower at Liverpool Airport. Sometime earlier a hangar and workshop had been built. The match works, owned by Bryant & May, can be seen at the top of the photograph to the right of the control tower.

New developments at Liverpool Corporation Airport. This aerial view of Liverpool Airport shows the new control tower, administrative offices and hangar. A radio beacon enabling aeroplanes to land safely at the airport at all times of the day and night, in all weather conditions, was part of the £250,000 scheme of development.

During the early years at Liverpool Airport, perhaps one of the most popular aircraft to land was the familiar sight of the British European Airways (BEA) Dakotas. The wheel stops ensured that they didn't run away too far!

Passengers leaving a BEA turbo-prop at Liverpool Airport and proceeding to the main administrative building.

The date 5 April 1950 marked the start of the Liverpool to London air service. Seen here inaugurating the service and giving a civic send off to a cargo of vaccine is the Lord Mayor of Liverpool, Alderman Cleary. The vaccine, from Evans Medical Supplies based in Speke, would arrive in London later that morning.

Speke Airport early in 1946. The scene shows a number of de Havilland aircraft on the apron. Speke Church can be seen in the middle of the horizon, and the Dunlop factory can also be seen to the right in the background.

A 'flying start' to a one day educational tour given to nineteen boys from a Liverpool school by British European Airways. Seen here leaving Liverpool Airport, the boys, together with their teachers, are ready for their first experience of flying. The flight would take them to Ringway Airport for a guided tour and then another exciting flight home.

Unloading a Bristol 170 Wayfairer freight plane of BKS Air Transport at Speke Airport, 1960. As the trade in air freight increased, the Bristol 170 Wayfairer became a common sight at the airport, especially when there was racing at Aintree. The Grand National attracted many horses from Ireland for which air transport was ideal.

A military aircraft lands at Speke. Although there weren't many military planes seen at the airport, there was an occasional landing. Officers are seen walking towards the main control tower and administrative centre.

For many years Liverpool Corporation Passenger Transport operated an exclusive service for airport passengers. This transported passengers between the airport and the city centre. Officials are seen here at the inauguration of the service in 1961.

The main entrance to Liverpool Airport, or Speke, as it was for many years. With the advent of jet travel, a new, longer, runway was needed. When the runway was built a new terminal building was also thought to be necessary. The grand entrance is still to be seen, but, sadly, no passengers. However, the building has now been renovated and refurbished and will open its doors once again, but this time as a luxury hotel!

A familiar sight at Speke Airport during the 1970s: a British Airways Viscount ready for boarding. Together with the very popular Dakotas, the most frequent visitor to Speke was the Viscount. Well wishers and the ever present plane spotters can be seen in the background. For many years the general public were allowed free access onto the viewing platform.

After the demise of the Dakota, the Vickers Viscount became the most popular plane to frequent the airport. Even now, the occasional Viscount touches down, but they're fast becoming collectors' items. The planes were very low when they flew over Brown & Bibby's (Brown, Bibby & Gregory, to give the firm its correct title), which is the factory in the background.

The team and officials of Liverpool Football Club returning home from another victorious foray into Europe! Bill Shankly is just at the bottom of the steps, but Ian Callaghan and Roger Hunt couldn't wait to get back on *terra firma* - they went ahead of the boss! Gerry Burne, Tommy Laurence, Tommy Smith and Gordon Milne are a little way behind 'Shanks', as are Peter Thompson, Peter Robinson and a very young-looking Bob Paisley.

Six
Speke at Work

Eastern Avenue was one of the last main roads to be built in Speke. However, not long after its construction, the road collapsed, and major road repairs were needed.

In 1960 a rash of technology broke out on the sides of some buses in Liverpool. Shift workers returning home late at night could be transported in style with an illuminated advertisement on the side of the bus. This view, taken on Speke Boulevard, shows an AEC bus with an advert for Walker's Pale Ale emblazoned along the side.

As late as 1955, Speke Boulevard was still a single carriageway road. With more industry being located in the estate and more people coming to live in the area, perhaps the time was fast approaching when the construction of a dual carriageway would become necessary. The landing lights for the airport can be seen on the right of the picture, with the 'prefabs' of Rycot Road behind them. Brown, Bibby & Gregory's factory can be seen on the left.

Road repairs being carried out along Eastern Avenue. Unfortunately, much of the road collapsed in February 1954.

Workman at Oglet Lane, at the commencement of the Hale Road improvement scheme.

The old Hale Road, with the No.82E making its way, eventually, to the Pier Head in Liverpool.

One of the busiest times of the day along Speke Boulevard was early in the morning. At that time workers going to Ford's, Evans Medical, Brown & Bibby's, Lockheed's and other factories on the Speke estate, were all intent on clocking-in on time! The No.500 bus was a new development. For a slightly higher fare, passengers who were in a hurry could board this limited stop bus. The journey between Speke and the centre of Liverpool, some eight miles away, was halved.

The factory owned by Brown, Bibby & Gregory employed many people from Speke. Their principal trade was the manufacture of cardboard boxes.

An aerial view of the Rootes' factory in April 1939. Throughout the duration of the Second World War this factory assembled aircraft for the war effort. All Saints Church can be seen at the bottom right, together with some of the new houses which were being built in the Dymchurch area of Speke.

Another aerial view of the Rootes' factory. All the aircraft components were shipped over from America in wooden cases and then assembled here. Following assembly, the aircraft were wheeled out onto the runway at Speke Airport and flown directly to their operational bases.

When this photograph was taken in 1951, the Rootes' factory had been taken over by the Dunlop Rubber Company. Instead of assembling aircraft, production was now changed to the manufacture of tyres. From this factory tyres of every shape and size were exported all over the world.

Firemen line up outside the fire station in All Saints Road for inspection. The fire station had originally been commissioned in 1940 as a temporary measure to cover the needs of the houses of Speke. However, as the centre of gravity of the new estate shifted, plans were approved in 1957 for an entirely new fire station to be built in Conleach Road, right in the centre of the estate. The new station was formally opened on 31 March 1960 by Mr H.M. Smith, Chief Inspector of Fire Services. Also in attendance at the ceremony were Alderman Louis Caplan and Alderman D. Cowley, respectively Chairman and Deputy Chairman of the Liverpool Fire Services Committee.

In the foreground is the original All Saints Road Fire Station. The parish church of All Saints can be seen in the background and to the left is the station office, located in a converted corporation house. In addition to the station office, there was a mess and some recreation facilities for the fire crews; sleeping accommodation was added later.

The Ford Motor Company. The body of the car begins to take shape in the body manufacture area, where the panels are welded together by hand spot welding and by large multi-welding machines capable of producing hundreds of spot welds simultaneously.

A general view of the Halewood press shop, 13 April 1965, showing some of the 103 gigantic presses which stamp out the hundreds of panels required to make a modern car.

One of the 200 quality control check points at the Ford Motor Company's factory at Halewood, 22 February 1965; an inspector is checking an Anglia body for gauge accuracy.

The inside of Evans Medical Supplies. The view shows a section of the filling room, where medicines and vaccines were packed.

Speke Hall Avenue, 23 February 1966, showing workers leaving the Dunlop factory at 3.00 pm when their shift ended. Security was always strict at the exits, following the apocryphal story of the worker who wheeled a car tyre out of the main gate. The story goes that he was caught by security staff; they followed the impressions which he was making in the snow all the way back to his car!

The Dunlop Rubber Company; a view of the giant cover-making section, looking south, May 1955. At that time Dunlop's was by far the largest employer in Speke. Several thousand people were employed on site and unemployment on the estate was a theoretical concept which most people hadn't even begun to contemplate.

The Distillers Company (Biochemicals) Limited, was situated half-way along Woodend Avenue, between Speke and Hunts Cross. Building started on the site in 1943, and the factory was in production by 1945. Penicillin and other significant drugs of the twentieth century have been developed and produced there.

Edwards Lane, mid-way between Speke and Hunts Cross, was a thriving, prosperous area in September 1946, as can be seen from the large number of cars in evidence. Many small to medium enterprises were based along here, often employing more than 100 staff. Some of the larger companies along the lane, including Meccano, employed well in excess of that number. Many staff were highly trained craftsmen, as a strong tradition of engineering skill was becoming established in the area.

Seven
Speke at Play

The tenements in Speke Road Gardens housed many young families so at weekends and during the summer holidays, the children's playground was very popular. The witch's hat, an all-time favourite, was always full.

Speke Park Recreation Ground. The opening ceremony was performed by the Lord Mayor of Liverpool on 7 July 1958.

The ever-popular children's playground in Roseheath Avenue, Halewood. Although Halewood wasn't built to emulate or rival Speke, there were many similar characteristics between the two developments. The planners still hadn't managed to break free of the tenement/maisonette concept.

Children playing at the 'Eight Ponds'. The ponds were later to become the site of the Ford factory at Halewood.

A catch! Sticklebacks and tadpoles were the main catch at the 'Eight Ponds'.

Children playing tug-of-war in the
grounds at Speke Hall.

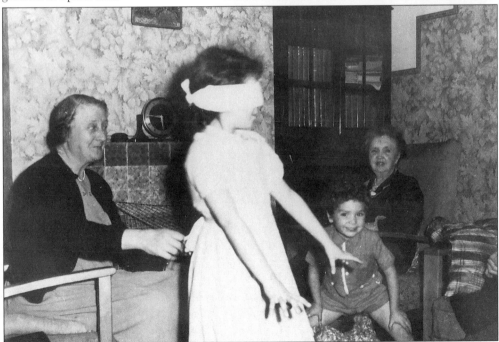

Playing Blind Man's Bluff, a popular Christmas game for families living in Speke. The room is
typical of the area and period with its family reference books and Bible in the book case, tiled
fire place and elaborate wallpaper featuring patterns and borders.

Speke had many youth organisations in the '40s and '50s, including the Girl Guides, Sea Scouts, Air Training Corps, Boys Brigade, Brownies, Cubs and Scouts. Seen here is the 16th Allerton Scout Band. Their services were often called upon to lead Scout parades and other civic ceremonies.

With the continuous and developing industrialisation of Speke, many works-led groups thrived. Seen here are the members of one of Dunlop's clubs enjoying a conducted tour around Liverpool Airport.

The top junior girls' class in Stocktonwood Road School, 1956-1957. Although sharing the same building - girls at one end, boys at the other - the girls' school and the boys' school were quite separate and even had their own teaching staff and headteacher. Along the upstairs corridor there was a white dividing line which served the purpose of separating the two schools, and 'woe betide' anybody who was caught crossing it. The punishment for crossing the line or other minor misdemeanours of this kind, was two strokes of the cane! The baby boom was reflected in the size of the classes. This particular class had forty-four on the register - nothing unusual at that time.

Stapleton Avenue Secondary Modern School for Boys Football Team, 1964.

Stocktonwood Road Infants School, Reception Class, 1957-1958.

Speke Baptist Church Sunday School group. By the mid '60s when this photograph was taken, attendance at the Sunday School had dropped quite considerably. Many younger families had now moved over to the new town of Runcorn.

Open air Sunday School, Speke Baptist Church. The Sunday School, complete with piano, was held throughout the month of July from 1962-1966. On the left in the background, the newly-built Central Shopping Parade can be seen, and, just to the right of that, Noah's Ark public house.

A group of Sunday School children at Speke Baptist Church, early '60s. At the time there were between fifty and sixty children who regularly attended the Sunday School. There was also a Bible class for older children.

The 12th Company Life Boy Team, Speke Baptist Church, 1958. Attendance at the meetings averaged between forty and fifty boys, all aged between 7 and 12. Later, most progressed to the Boys Brigade, which was also based at the church.

Jack Alger as Superman, seen here on one of the floats in the annual Dunlop's carnival. The carnival was quite an event in Speke and, although resources were scarce, because of the efforts expended by all of the participants, it was always a great success within the wider community.

Knobbly knees competition; another social event in the Dunlop's Work Study Department's calendar.

During the Second World War there was a number of US air bases not too far away from Speke. A few years after, many young ladies decided to become GI brides and emigrated to the USA. Seen here being presented with 'a small token of our appreciation' is Miss Peggy Ryan before leaving Dunlop's for the USA in 1952.

After working in Dunlop's for many years there were also numerous retirement parties.

Another leaving 'do' at Dunlop's in the early '50s. Commodities and cash were still hard come by, hence the 'token' gift.

St Christopher's Players, formed in 1955, was open to all parishioners and their friends who were aged over 18. Meetings were held in the junior school. The John Bull printing had its limitations, but nevertheless, the productions were very popular. *The Song of Bernadette*, performed in the spring of 1958 was particularly successful.

Performance of St Christopher's Players in a production of *Caesar's Friend*, late '50s. The players were performing for a period of about ten years to packed houses. Everybody's aunt came and 'all the girls from work'.

The Rose Queen, Kathleen Harvey, together with her full retinue posing outside of the infants school at Stocktonwood Road. With the Second World War having only just come to an end, there was a particularly patriotic theme in Rose Queen Festivals for a few years afterwards.

The Deputy Lord Mayor and Deputy Lady Mayoress of Liverpool at the crowning of the Speke Rose Queen Ceremony, 1944-1945. The Rose Queen, Kathleen Harvey, is seen here with the retiring queen, Edna Frazer. The robes for the Rose Queen, the retiring Rose Queen and the Rose Bowl for the event were provided by Speke Central Committee - a group of people who organised many social and cultural events in Speke throughout the year.

Daisy Grice on her way to be crowned as Speke's Rose Queen for 1945-1946, seen here preceded by her retinue and herald. The procession moved from the playground of the infants school at Stocktonwood Road, to the balcony area in the junior school, which was on the same site. In the background can be seen the boys from the band of St Edward's Orphanage, Stoneycroft, who provided much of the musical entertainment during the afternoon.

Daisy Grice being crowned Speke's Rose Queen, 1945-1946, by the Lady Mayoress of Liverpool. The crowning ceremony took place in the boys' wing of Stocktonwood Road School. On the playing fields behind the school a festival fair was always held, with swingboats, roundabouts and music.

Another sunny day for the crowning of Speke's Rose Queen; summers were always long and hot in those days! In 1946-1947 Rhiannon Hughes was crowned queen, and Daisy Grice was the retiring queen. This immediate post-war patriotic scene, with Britannia, Liberty and Peace in the tableau, was taken in the junior boys' playground of Stocktonwood Road School.

The Spirit of Victory! A scene at one of the many street parties which were held in Speke. As the vicar, Revd W.H. Wade, said in his letter in the *Speke Messenger* of June 1945, 'I was impressed, in my visits to innumerable parties, etc., by the general and commendable restraint of Speke people and by the desire to make our spontaneous celebrations worthy of the community. The bonfire parties, tea-parties and the sole-destroying dancing in the streets till early morning brought neighbours together as never before. Many spoke to and danced with those with whom they had before scarcely had nodding acquaintance.'

Many arrangements for coronation parties had to be changed at short notice when it started to rain! This photograph shows some youngsters crammed into the 'parlour' ready to enjoy their party.

There was a special souvenir copy of the *Speke Messenger* published in June 1945, price 6d. In addition to the usual contents of the magazine, which included the vicar's letter, the Liverpool Diocesan leaflet, an update of the parish register and the standard pages of advertisements for local tradesmen and providers of other services, including, very fittingly, the local undertaker, there were special articles on the *Growing Community Life* and a *Short History of Speke Church*.

The Speke Messenger   June, 1945

The Message of the Cover

"In this Sign—Conquer."

Victory in Europe has caused the sword of war to be broken. It has served its purpose of defence, and that of liberation from one of the cruellest tyrannies the world has ever known.

The energy and self-sacrifice that has won the victory under God must now be used to remake the world. For this we must use another weapon. The sword must go through a miraculous change in texture and use.

This is taking place—for the hilt is turning into wood. Its complete metamorphosis has not yet been made, for war is still raging in the Far East, and men's hearts are still full of hatred. The shaft of the sword therefore still remains steel.

As Christians we must continue to pray that the time may soon come when the Cross of Jesus shall be our only weapon—our symbol—our inspiration. That the war may become one not of physical but of spiritual power, and that the banner of the victorious Saviour may be upheld in every land.

> Onward, Christian Soldiers, marching as to war,
> With the Cross of Jesus, going on before.

SOUVENIR COPY   SIXPENCE

The message on the cover was entitled 'In this Sign - Conquer'. The article exhorted Christians to continue to pray for a time when war would be no more. In 1945 the circulation of the *Messenger* was approaching 1,500 copies per month.

Geraldine Groves on her Triang tricycle in Oglet Lane, mid 1940s. Directly in front of her, on the beach, were several rows of pyramid-shaped 'tank traps'. During and immediately after the Second World War, there was a girdle of defences around Speke - just in case the enemy should wish to sabotage the aircraft factory.

The walk on Sunday afternoon was obligatory. Here a family at journey's end sat on the beech at Oglet. Every working class man wore a trilby in those days, often at a jaunty angle. It was also important to wear a 'mac' with the collar flicked up.

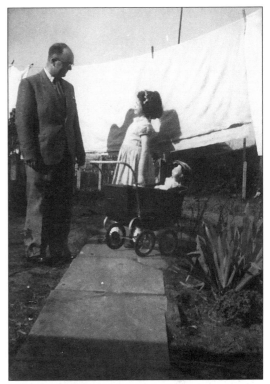

Monday lunchtime in the back garden and a proud daughter tells her father of the events of the morning. It must be lunchtime because he is at home, and it must be Monday because the washing's on the line!

Relatives often visited on Sundays. It was a difficult journey out to Speke from the suburbs of Liverpool and Sunday was especially difficult because a restricted bus service operated then.

Speke Central Committee, 1944. The committee organised several events and clubs in Speke including the annual parade and Crowning of the Speke Rose Queen Ceremony, the Gardening Club, various dances throughout the year, the Youth Club, the Dramatic Society, the Wednesday Guild, and the Poultry Club!

Rootes Securities, Staff Supervision Dinner, 6 October 1944. Rootes made aircraft and other munitions throughout the Second World War; the factory was later owned by the Dunlop Rubber Co. Ltd.

Eight

Around Speke

The old Hunts Cross Hotel. This site is now the home of Kwik Save, with the new Hunts Cross Hotel built a little further back. The old garage can be seen further along from the hotel. The road's just a little busier today!

This view shows Woodend Lane as was (now Woodend Avenue), leading towards the village of Speke. The building to the right of the view is the Hunts Cross Hotel and the road which goes to the left is now Hillfoot Avenue.

Looking across the junction towards the road to Woolton. On the right can be seen the old Hunts Cross Hotel and, a little further back just by the telegraph pole, is Hunts Cross railway station.

This is a view of Hillfoot Avenue, Hunts Cross, on 25 June 1938. Although the road carried very little vehicular traffic at that time, it was still constructed as a dual carriageway - enlightened planning?

A more recent photograph of Hunts Cross in 1969, showing the shops at the centre. Traffic lights have now been erected and an indication of the developing affluence of the area can be seen from the new Ford Anglia estate car in the foreground. All the models in the Anglia range of cars were built just down the road in Ford's factory at Halewood.

Scene looking from Hillfoot Avenue, Hunts Cross, towards the roundabout at the junction between the continuation of Hillfoot Avenue, going towards Hunts Cross to the left, and Speke Hall Avenue, going towards Speke on the right. The roundabout has now been replaced by traffic lights. The Asda store entrance is now on the extreme right of the picture but is not shown here, as the photograph was taken on 11 August 1947.

A new road and houses being built at Yew Tree Road (Mackets Lane), Hunts Cross, 7 August 1936.

Access to the new shops in Mackets Lane could have been made easier!

In 1954, when this was taken, it was difficult for shoppers in Mackets Lane to pick their way through the puddles when it rained; the road has now been re-surfaced!

The new shops in Mackets Lane, 7 August 1936.

Hunts Cross Station, Cheshire Lines Committee, between the wars with four platforms evident. The line was inaugurated on 1 March 1873. The station, which is still very busy, was opened in May 1874. In 1883 the station was rebuilt to accommodate the quadrupling of lines.

Mackets Lane, Hunts Cross, 23 February 1953.

Tombstone of the Childe of Hale, Hale churchyard. A portrait of the Childe of Hale is on permanent display in Brasenose College, Oxford. Around the frame of the painting is the following inscription: 'This is the true Portraiture of John Middleton the Childe of Hale, who was borne at Hale 1578, and dyede 1623, height 9 feet 3 inches.'

Lighthouse, Hale, near Liverpool.

Hale lighthouse on the upper reaches of the Mersey Estuary, marking the bend of the river on the way to Widnes and Warrington. (*Liverpool Evening Express*, 9 May 1939).

Hale lighthouse. At this point, known as Hale Head, the River Mersey is at its widest - almost three miles across. The width of the river here also makes it extremely shallow. In earlier times the crossing at this point to Weston in Cheshire was known as the old Hale Ford. Many stories are told of precarious and even tragic crossings. The Ford was used regularly until late into the nineteenth century, when a bridge was built across the river at Widnes.

West view of the gatehouse to the Old Hutte, now classed as part of Halewood, 1870.

The gatehouse, seen in the 1940s.

Painting entitled *Ye Childe of Hale* (1578-1623) for a hotel sign, 1929. This was the finished sign before it was erected on the Childe of Hale Hotel, Hale.

Erecting *Ye Childe of Hale* sign outside the Hale Hotel. The painting of the sign was completed in September 1929.

A general view of some of the cottages in the village of Hale, taken on 13 November 1934, although the cottages themselves were built in the sixteenth century.

The Childe of Hale's cottage is still standing in the village. It is somewhat different from many of the other cottages, in that, 'it is to be noticed that the beams which in other cottages form the ceiling, are wanting here; the roof, which is plastered and whitewashed, forms the ceiling, and this gives to the room a very lofty appearance to which the small low door contrasts strangely.'

The very edge of Speke and the outskirts of Hale. This photograph, taken in 1951, looks from Hale, along Hale Road, to the estate of Speke in the distance.

The cross in the centre of Hale village. As the sign clearly indicates, Liverpool was a few miles along the road to the right, but first the traveller had to pass through Speke, about a mile away.

Hale Hall, built in the fifteenth century is shown here in August 1937 in an advanced state of decay. The hall was demolished later that year.

On 12 April 1937, the following notification of auction was reported in the *Daily Post*: 'The Hale Estate of 2,770 freehold acres adjoining the Liverpool city boundary and the Speke estate, and having four miles of frontage to the river Mersey, is to be offered at auction... This estate, promising a splendid building area, comprises nineteen mixed farms, a number of smallholdings, seventy-seven cottages and houses, including the famous home of the 'Childe of Hale', commercial woodlands, etc..' The estate was purchased by the Fleetwood-Hesketh family. Mr Peter Fleetwood-Hesketh, who moved to the village in 1947, lived in Hale Manor House, seen here. The dwelling was formally the Parsonage.

A rare sight in Hale - the killing of a fox. Foxes were not common in Hale during the '50s when this was taken.

Members of Hale Youth Club attending the village fete, *c.* 1952. The youngsters had been asked to represent the many different sporting activities that were practised in the village. Club members can be seen dressed as football players, tennis players and even one as a speedway rider.

Many ancient traditions are still observed in the village of Hale. The Lord Mayor of Hale is invested in the Childe of Hale Hotel and he has several officers, including the Keeper of the Mayor's Purse, the Keeper of the Records, the Mace-bearer, the Town Crier and the Sword-bearer. The Freemen of Hale are also appointed at this time and take or renew their ancient oaths.

Pictured before the farm implement sale in 1938, is Mr Frederick Bent of Heath Gate Farm.

Pupils at Hale School in the 1920s. The children walked to Hale Park where this photograph was taken. Miss Fox was the class teacher.

An old photograph of Hale at the turn of the century. At this time, the roads were little more than wide tracks.

Cottages along the Dungeon in Hale. When the Hale Estate became part of the Speke Estate, the lane became known as Dungeon Lane.

Richard White's breaker's yard was at the bottom of the Dungeon in Hale. Seen here is the *Manora*, one of the last sailing ships to be broken up at the yard. On the same site, Mr Prince rented premises where he made fireworks. He then sold them to the villagers of Hale and Speke.